# HOW TO BONK
# AT WORK

*"Solus dilectio qualitas"*

Authors' dedication:
To Bill Clinton, who doubtless regrets that this book was not published earlier…

WARNING
Prion books declines all responsibility for any problems you might encounter while using this book at your workplace, i.e. pregnant boss, broken office after getting carried away with a secretary, your colleagues' jealousy because you've bonked everyone in your company… We are not responsible.*

This edition published in 2010 by Prion Books
an imprint of The Carlton Publishing Group
20 Mortimer Street
London W1T 3JW

ISBN 978-1-85375-799-0

A catalogue record of this book can be obtained from the British Library

Editorial Manager: Roland Hall
Design: Emily Clarke, Gulen Shevki Taylor, Sailesh Patel
Production Controller: Claire Hayward

Printed in Italy

5 7 9 10 8 6 4

* But we will be proud of you!

# HOW TO BONK AT WORK

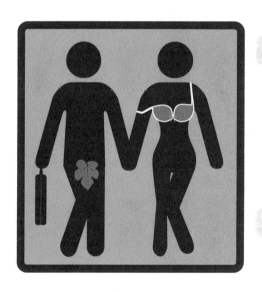

## MATS & ENZO

# CONTENTS

# INTRODUCTION

## Why don't you love your job?

It's the same thing every day: you don't want to go to work. Like so many you probably think that the reasons for this are your idiot boss, your boring job, lack of appreciation, small salary... But you are wrong. While all these things play a certain role in your perception of work, it is, in fact, a very minor role.

You might not want to admit it to yourself, but the only true reason you hate your job is, in one word: SEX. Yes, sex! As surprising as this may seem, the fact that nobody in modern society dares to openly address is that a general lack of sex at work is the main cause of internal disquiet of employees.

Why? Simply because the very primitive need for sex is written into the deepest corners of our genes, but it is constantly blocked by company rules that don't allocate places for sex at work, which leads to incredible frustration.

## Achieving happiness at work: a very simple answer

**Bonk at work basic law**

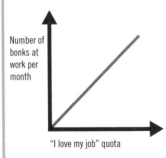

Number of bonks at work per month

"I love my job" quota

A recent American study has shown that we have been looking for sources of happiness and contentment at work in all the wrong places. The happiness of employees is not linked to the size of their pay check or recognition for their work, but simply to the number of opportunities to bonk at work. Stanley Debite, the global authority on workplace bonking, has very clearly identified the direct link between bonking at work and happiness at work (see left).

## Office life offers incredible bonking opportunities

If it is true that work is largely inconvenient (it is so much more amusing to have drinks with your buddies, go line fishing or knit a lovely cardigan), it also has a unique advantage: a vast pool of potential co-bonkers, accessible all day long, all looking for a way to escape the workplace ennui.

However, as ample as is the offer of potential shag partners, they are not immediately available. It will not suffice to say: "Uh, fancy a bonk in my office?" to be able to bonk right there and then. Moreover, the group of people you would like to bonk is never the same as the group of people who would actually bonk you. For example: you would love to bonk the new intern or the cute PR girl, but do they want to bonk you? And don't forget that many other colleagues would happily bonk your firm's hottest employees just as much as you.

Let's face it: the colleagues who would be willing to bonk you on the spot might not be the ones you are attracted to, as they probably weigh over 330 pounds and haven't done it for years.

## How do you navigate this collective lust?

**Work frustration explained**

Colleagues you would like to bonk

Colleagues you can bonk

This gap between the people you want to bonk and those who would bonk you creates what we call "frustration at work". We will help you eliminate this frustration with our *Bonk at Work* manual. It will let you bonk all the colleagues you are attracted to in your company. Yes, you can!

## Read this book and start bonking at work tomorrow!

Bonking at work is considered dangerous. While it is true that it can raise many questions, it is also true that contrary to popular belief it is far from impossible. The problem is that too many think with their bits rather than with their brain. They need to understand that bonking at work is actually not just about bonking.

To give you a hand in your bonking adventures at work, we decided it was high time we wrote a practical guide on how to safely navigate between office sex and your career. A challenging task, but one we believe we have succeeded in rather splendidly. In the following pages we are presenting you with countless solutions and ideas that will shake up your work life forever.

We have decided to unveil everything for you: the best bonk places, the best positions adapted to your work equipment and, of course, the solutions to all problems that you might encounter during your workplace bonk – an activity that is far from being risk free if one is not well versed in it.

This book will let you discover how to jump into the Infinite Loop of Workplace Bonking. This is a powerful system that will allow you to bonk at work more than you ever imagined possible.

**Start**

## THE EXPERT: Stanley Debite

Stanley Debite has a well-established reputation as the foremost expert in the matter of workplace bonking. His rise has been more than impressive. Despite never finishing high school, he has managed to go from being a simple employee to becoming the CEO of a multinational company. For the past ten years his exclusive lectures on "Bonking at Work" have been an immense success in the United States, despite the $2,000 entry fee per participant. In these lectures he unveils his BFS (Bonk for Success) method, which is appreciated by all who want to know how to use their... equipment at work. He always finishes his lectures with his famous "Yes we bonk!" slogan, which of course was the inspiration behind Barack Obama's presidential campaign motto. Stanley Debite is also Obama's personal coach on the subject matter and was coaching all other American presidents on bonking in the workplace, with the notable exception of Bill Clinton.

Very conscious of professional ethics, Stanley Debite never tried to financially profit from his notoriety through commercial endeavours. *The Economist* recently revealed that he refused a $1m offer to create an office sex toy brand bearing his name; he also refused numerous offers to serve as artistic adviser in different pornographic films based in a work environment. He is holding true to his motto: "Quality Bonk Only", and wants to make the study of workplace bonking a scientific discipline in its own right, much like Communications or Finance.

We are honoured to work with such an expert. His wise and exclusive advice will impress you.

**BONK FOR SUCCESS**

a step-by-step approach to bonking

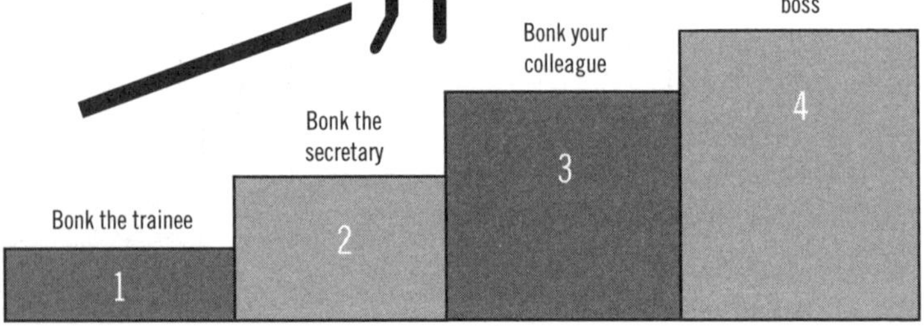

Bonk your boss

Bonk your colleague

Bonk the secretary

Bonk the trainee

1

2

3

4

# PART 1: FOR A GOOD START

Just as you wouldn't go deep-sea diving without at least some basic knowledge, you can't start bonking at work without preparation. We will therefore begin by explaining eight basic concepts.

# THE BASIC RULES

**Rule 1:** Before you begin bonking at work, locate all security cameras, identify when the postman, the cleaners and the "How about a cuppa?" guy make their rounds.

**Rule 2:** Wear clothes you can quickly remove and put back on. Ideally you will invest in a suit or skirt with press studs that can be taken off in a matter of seconds, much like the trousers favoured by male strippers.

**Rule 3:** When bonking at work, begin with positions that you have already tested in the safety of your own home. Try new positions only after you have studied the Bonkasutra chapter in depth.

**Rule 4:** After getting dressed in a hurry, always check that you haven't put on a wrong piece of clothing. Example: your colleague's blouse or worse, her skirt; even worse - your underpants over your trousers.

**Rule 5:** When properly dressed, check that you don't have any traces of the bonk in visible places: lipstick smudged around your ears, hickeys...

**Rule 6:** Acknowledge defeat when you are caught in the act and don't try to invent reasons why you and your colleague are naked in your office without having read this book first. You will just look pathetic.

Once you learn these basics, you can continue to the study of the PCB method.

## The PCB: the best way to bonk!

We created a special method that will help you bonk your office mates: the PCB (PLAN - CHECK - BONK).

Carefully tested in the field for five years, the PCB is the method that will help you bonk the maximum number of colleagues with minimal risks. It is of crucial importance you understand that our bonk method is based on detailed planning prior to each bonk, and a careful check of the site to see if it is adapted to bonking.

If you want to bonk safely and not get caught mid-bonk by a colleague or – worse – your boss, scrupulously follow the proportions we suggest: in one hour allocated for sex at work with a colleague, spend 30 minutes (50%) imagining and conceiving your bonk (place, positions, partner...). Don't hesitate to prepare a 3D bonk simulation on your computer or, if you are not a geek, with dolls (Working Woman Barbie and Businessman Ken are especially adapted for this).

Once you have your bonk plan memorized, check the chosen bonk spot in detail (30%). Note the comings and goings of your colleagues. Finally, use the remaining 12 minutes to bonk. If you have to remember only one of all the mind-boggling pieces of advice in this book, it would be PCB. Or in other words: never bonk without a plan and a very detailed prior examination of the chosen bonk spot.

Such time allocation is important whatever your bonk level. After approximately one year of regular workplace bonking, you can allot a part of the check time to bonking. But keep in mind, dangers lurk everywhere and no bonker, expert or beginner is immune to them if he/she doesn't respect the PCB.

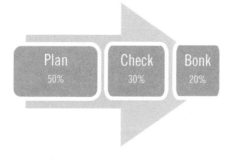

## Carefully select your bonk partner

Finding a hot colleague to bonk seems easy, but you have to know how to go about it. As you have surely noticed already, all departments in your company are not equally blessed with good-looking men and women. If you seek in bad places, you will find it extremely difficult to find an acceptable bonk partner.

### Where to find hot colleagues

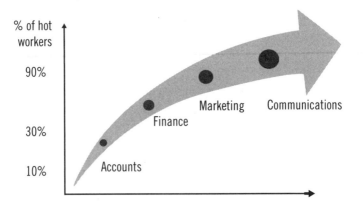

What causes such distribution in a company? Everyone knows that the hotties are naturally drawn to jobs like flight attendant, nurses or communications. The same holds true for hot guys. This is why you most often find good-looking employees in such positions. Moreover, if a hot girl or guy makes a youthful mistake and decides to study accounting, he or she will later, when employed in a company, naturally evolve towards Finance, then Marketing and finally the Communications department, the natural habitat of all sexy employees in a company. (See example on the next page for hot colleague migration in a company.)

# Bonk partner selection!

**Understanding the migration of hot colleagues in the firm**

Hot colleague hire

Accounts          Finance          Marketing          Communications

You now understand that you can't go bonk hunting with your eyes to the ground. Keep your eyes open permanently, be open to possibilities that you could never foresee and think of how to bonk colleagues with whom you rub elbows every day. Be patient and careful, but don't take too long – after a certain amount of time you will accept just about anyone, as shown in the diagram below.

**The basic law of bonking at work**

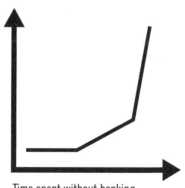

% of your colleagues you wouldn't mind bonking

Time spent without bonking

# Work–bonk etiquette

Here are five rules you should never forget:

**Rule 1:**  Never bonk a colleague you know is a superior's ex (same rule that applies to bonking your friend's ex).

**Rule 2:**  Don't explain all the details of a bonk to your colleagues. A simple "I've bonked her/him" is enough.

**Rule 3:**  If two people book the boardroom to bonk at the same time, the higher ranking person will have it (if they both plan to bonk the same person, they can all enter at the same time).

**Rule 4:**  If a bonker forgets the name of the person he/she bonked the day before, his/her closest colleagues will help find the name by searching through the photos on the Intranet.

**Rule 5:**  Never compare bonk numbers within a company and, of course, never organize bonk competitions within a company.

## Who can bonk the intern?

While we were preparing this book, an unusually high number of our contacts asked us the same question: "You who know how to bonk at work, tell me who can bonk the intern?" Since the new intern is, of course, everyone's prey we decided to dedicate a paragraph to this. Since the beginning of internships and interns in companies, an implicit law gives priority to employees in higher

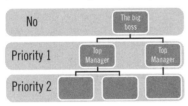

positions in bonking the intern. It is only if your superiors don't show any interest in them that you can try to seduce him/her into a bonk. There is, however, one notable exception in this: the big boss never bonks an intern. You now have a good basis for workplace bonking, but it will be of no use to you if you don't know the art of seduction at work. We therefore present the P.L.A.T.E ® method…

# The method of irresistible seduction

We studied a group of 1,500 employees to find seduction methods that work. We found that there are five prevailing attitudes that are crucial in the process. You can internalize them with the help of the P.L.A.T.E ® method.

P - Powerful. It's a fact: women like powerful men and men seem to enjoy seducing women most when they are not easily accessible. The higher you climb in the company, the more opportunities to bonk you will have. Here are some numbers that will help you better understand: a FTSE 100 manager has about eight propositions to bonk in the course of one day, a warehouse employee gets one every 12 years. You should therefore not hesitate to lie about your position to a colleague you wish to bonk. Say, for example: "Yes, you see, I am responsible for emptying all the rubbish bins of the company. I am the most important link in the chain. Without me the whole company would be in the toilet. Basically only the big boss is more important than me."

L - Luxurious. You have to make your colleagues believe that you have lots of money and that you know how to spend it. Wear expensive clothes, and if you can't afford them, multiply your clothes' real price by 100. The sneakers or a skirt that you bought at the market for £5 will become a rare collectors' item worth at least £500. Also play up your car. Say, for example: "You know, the Lada that I drive is the trendiest car at the moment." Do this for all other objects you own: your multicolour pen, your whistle key chain... The more you impress them, the sooner they will agree to bonk you.

A - Artistic. Women love men with artistic souls and men like women to be more cultured than they are. You must therefore exhibit artistic qualities, even if your job has nothing to do with art. Here are some things you can do: Randomly colour each cell in your Excel document in pink, yellow and red. Proudly show off your choice of colours to everyone. If your colleagues ask you what you did this weekend, tell them you saw the latest John Batt exhibit (a famous neo-artist), even if in fact you only took your car to the carwash, wearing your sweatpants.

T - Tall. Blame women's reproductive instincts that women are generally drawn to tall and strong blokes, while women can blame it on male models that being tall is one of the key sex-appeal criteria. If you are below 1.8 m (6 ft), walk on the tips of your toes when colleagues of interest approach you. Wear high heels (yes, blokes too – it worked for Sarkozy didn't it?) As for clothes, buy children's clothing and wear it on the days when you have meetings where interesting colleagues will be present. If they point out that your sleeves only come to your elbows, explain to them: "Yes, I know; this is because I am so tall, I can never find clothes my size."

E - Expert. You should be perceived as the dominant male or the alpha female. The best way to achieve this is to keep saying all over the company that you are an expert. You don't have to be an expert in something complicated; you can just say, for example: "I am the best at making 3D graphics in Excel" or "I am the expert in CRRPL..." (even if it doesn't stand for anything). You should also be well versed in all subjects pertaining to cats and horses. You can then use any opportunity to insert them into conversation, for example: "It's interesting that you mention Morocco – did you know that it's seventh on the list of countries with most cats in the world?"

## Seduction: The Deodorant Law

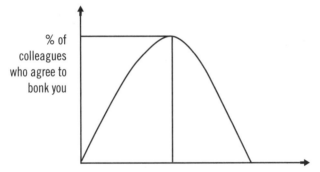

% of colleagues who agree to bonk you

Quantity of deodorant you put on in the morning

At work, no deodorant = no bonk. However, if you empty half of the bottle on yourself each morning and people can smell you at 500 m (1,640 ft) away = no bonk for you either. Same holds true for excessive perfume use.

Experiment beforehand to find the optimal quantity of deodorant and/or perfume that will maximize your bonk opportunities. Make an Excel chart to optimize your results.

# The real risk: getting caught!

Having sex at work is really not all that difficult. It is rather like what you already do at home when you are feeling naughty and bonk outside your bed. The main problem with bonking at work comes from the constant danger of getting caught. To help you better understand which situations can lead to being seen, we researched this problem carefully. It turns out that in 60% of cases the employees were caught by one or several colleagues, in 20% of cases by their boss and 15% were stupidly caught because, in the excitement of the moment, they forgot about surveillance cameras. The remaining 5% were cases of exhibitionism.

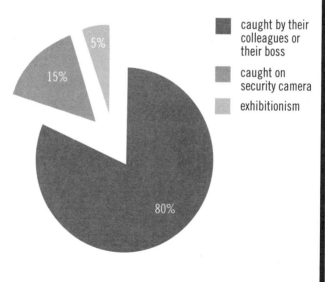

How office bonkers get caught

- caught by their colleagues or their boss
- caught on security camera
- exhibitionism

# PART 2: WHERE TO BONK AT WORK

Where to bonk? How to figure out if a certain place is a good bonk spot? How to make it exciting by choosing a good spot?

You will find out in the following pages that it is possible to do better than secretly bonk in a disused office deep underground.

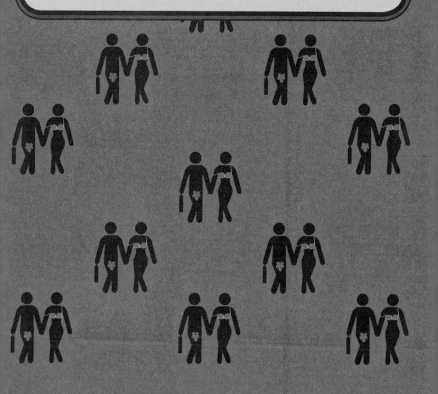

## The Adrenaline Law

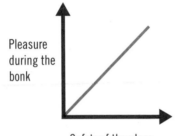

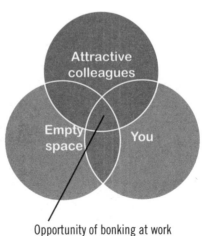

## COFFEE MACHINE

Quick bonk: ★★★★★
Long bonk: ★
Group bonk: ★★★★★

## Expert advice

"When you have a regular partner, there are of course many better places. However, if you meet a person who sparks your interest, invite him/her for coffee or tea, chat for five minutes and then say: 'I can give you a quick bonk now if you fancy.' This has worked more than once for me – give it a go."

## Pros & cons

+ Bonking is much more relaxing than just having coffee or tea.
+ A wonderful place for some convivial bonking between colleagues.
+ The caffeine can give you the stamina that will be especially appreciated if it's your first bonk.
- If your colleagues see you going towards the coffee room, they might join you.
- 99% chance of getting caught by a colleague who comes for a coffee.
- If you bonk hard on the coffee machine, your colleagues might not appreciate it.

## When to go there?

All day, but avoid the hour after the lunch break.

# YOUR OFFICE

Quick bonk: ★★★★★
Long bonk: ★★★★★
Group bonk: ★★★★★

## Expert advice

"Your office is the ideal place for your first workplace bonk. In this safe environment you will hear the steps of colleagues before they knock on your door. Some advice: use the same precautions that you exercise when you turn your computer monitor away from the immediate gaze of anyone entering, and make sure that your furniture is carefully and strategically placed so that you can't be immediately spotted bonking. This will give you a few precious seconds to dress quickly."

## Pros & cons

+ We are always best when playing on our home turf.
+ You can hide sex toys in the drawers and turn the many office devices into naughty accessories.
+ You can spend a great part of your day plotting your bonk and strategically preparing the area.
- Crumpled paper all over your desk and your office upside-down afterwards.
- Serious risk of breaking the office equipment that your company has supplied you with.
- No real possibilty that could make it risky and therefore more exciting.

## When to go there?

All day except during the hours when the cleaning staff do their rounds.

# THE OPEN SPACE

Quick bonk: ★★★
Long bonk: ★
Group bonk: ★★★★★

## Expert advice

"If you are in a budding relationship with a colleague, don't wait for the rumour mill to expose your romance. Use the open space to consummate your relationship. Bonk him or her on your desk; it is an opportunity to show your incredible skills to your colleagues, which can come in handy in the future."

## Pros & cons

+ If you bonk under a desk, the overall noise in the open space will mask your bonking noises.
+ A randy colleague will never be far away.
+ A cornucopia of available material and ample space for extraordinary group bonks.
- A randy colleague is almost never the attractive colleague.
- In a particularly large, open space you risk not noticing a colleague who could be observing, filming or – worse – attempt to join you.
- If you work in an IT company, you are exposed to disturbing situations with 10 men for 1 woman in the event of a group bonk.

## When to go there?

Take advantage of the lunch break (12–2 pm).

## THE PARKING GARAGE

Quick bonk: ★★★★★
Long bonk: ★★★
Group bonk: ★★

## Expert advice

"When I was younger I converted a van and made it into a Bonkmobile: pink handles to assist in performing different positions, tinted windows, velvet curtains, glove compartment full of condoms, chilled champagne bucket... and a king size mattress in the back. I suggest to all the readers who would like to take full advantage of this book to invest in one. After reading this advice, you will see all your minivan driving colleagues in a very different light..."

## Pros & cons

+ Possibility to pick up a souvenir video of your exploits from security.
+ An unlit space where shy people lose their inhibitions.
+ If your car is too small or if you don't want to get it dirty, you can use a colleague's car.
- The number of partners you can fit into the car and the positions you can carry out depend on the size of your car (the car model bonk law).
- Parking garages are often dirty, and not conducive to parking your exposed bum anywhere in it.
- Probably not the fairytale spot your bonkee dreamt of.

## When to go there?

All day except during arrivals and departures (8–9 am and 5–6 pm).

## THE CORRIDOR

Quick bonk: ★★★★★
Long bonk: ★
Group bonk: ★

## Expert advice

"To all you premature ejaculators out there: bonk in the corridor! Your problem becomes a highly appreciated advantage there..."

## Pros & cons

+ The possibility to use the fire extinguisher to put out a colleague who is on fire.
+ Possibility to do a doggy-style snake bonk the length of the corridor.
+ The constant passing of colleagues and the absence of possible hiding places make this dangerous zone a terribly exciting place.
- Limited material for various positions (fire extinguishers, frames...).
- Long bonks only possible at night.
- The worn-out rug can cause you pain (knees, back...).

## When to go there?

The most adventurous should go during the day, before everyone arrives (8 am), while all others are advised to opt for the end of the day (5–6 pm).

# THE STOCK ROOM / WAREHOUSE

Quick bonk: ★★★★
Long bonk: ★★★
Group bonk: ★★★

## Expert advice

"A few years ago I fooled around with a short girl – 1.4 m (4 ft 8 in) – but our height difference created some issues. I have since passed the forklift operator test. It allows me to lift my partner to the ideal height.
Knowing how to manage a pallet truck also allows you to lift heavier ladies."

## Pros & cons

+ Completely empty and available at the end of the day.
+ The abundance of different objects will let you spice up your sexual relations.
+ Stock rooms are filled with cardboard boxes of all sizes that can be used to create a little cardboard hut for bonking.
- If you fall asleep in a carton after making love you risk being shipped across the globe.
- Men: danger of getting impaled by a palette truck while doing it doggy style.
- You could be accused of breaking and entering if caught.

## When to go there?

After 4 pm.

# THE MEETING ROOM

Quick bonk: ★★★
Long bonk: ★★★
Group bonk: ★★★★★

## Expert advice

"I would suggest saving the meeting room for group bonks. Book the meeting room on the Intranet and send a mass e-mail with 'team building' as the subject to invite everyone for a group bonk. For once, everyone will leave the meeting room more relaxed than when they entered. A real bonus for you *and* your company!"

## Pros & cons

+ The meeting table will become your king size bed.
+ Possibility to use the projector to screen a porno while bonking.
+ Possibility to film and simultaneously view your bonk with the projector.

- It is increasingly difficult to book meeting rooms.
- Meeting rooms often have glass walls or large windows which could lure your voyeuristic colleagues.
- Due to the popularity of this bonk spot, someone could already be bonking under the table when you enter.

## When to go there?

All day.

# BOSS'S OFFICE

Quick bonk: ★★★★★
Long bonk: ★
Group bonk: ★

## Expert advice

"The easiest way to gain access to your boss's office is to bonk your boss, which is what I would recommend for the first time. Once you gain confidence, go and bonk there as often as possible… without the boss!"

## Pros & cons

+ Possibility to use the golden or silver sex toys in his or her drawer.
+ Nobody will bother you because nobody comes in to disturb the boss.
+ The feeling of power mixed with the elation that comes from a good bonk.
- You risk trouble in case you break your boss's PC or desk.
- You will be in trouble if your partner finds out that you're not really the boss.
- Careful when role playing: games such as "the mean boss and the sultry secretary" could lead to misunderstandings and even accusations of sexual harassment.

## When to go there?

When the boss is away… or not!

# THE LIFT

Quick bonk: ★★★★★
Long bonk: ★
Group bonk: ★★

## Expert advice

"Personally I am a fan of external lifts with glass walls. When I bonk in this type of lift, I feel like a Superman bonker because I feel like I'm flying!"

## Pros & cons

+ The erotic feeling of being in a mirrored cage.
+ The handles facilitate more acrobatic positions.
+ A great place for elevating bonking opportunities with someone you don't know.
- It can get crowded if more than seven people are involved.
- The unpleasant possibility of being interrupted when someone gets the lift.
- The danger of getting stuck inside for hours with an ugly colleague who will see this as an opportunity to bonk you.

## When to go there?

Avoid the hours of arrivals and departures (8-9 am and 5-6 pm).

# THE PHOTOCOPIER

Quick bonk: ★★★★★
Long bonk: ★
Group bonk: ★★★

## Expert advice

"Everyone needs it at one time or another, which makes it a great place to meet people from other departments. Here you will meet pretty assistants and beautiful secretaries, and also busy managers who need to make a quick copy. This is my favourite meeting place. I make over 350 useless copies a day, just to meet new people."

## Pros & cons

+ Convenient for flirting, and flirting can often lead to a hot bonk in the office of one of the two employees.
+ Possibility to propose a group bonk among strangers to kill time if there is a queue.
+ The heat of the copy machine useful to get a colleague hot.
- The glass of the copy machine can break and your buttocks can get stuck.
- Risk of e-mailing a copy of your intimate parts to the whole company if you press the wrong button during a bonk on the copy machine.
- The overheating of the machine can lead to serious injuries and embarrassing situations.

## When to go there?

Avoid going outside office hours.

# THE TOILET

Quick bonk: ★★★★★
Long bonk: ★★★★
Group bonk: ★

## Expert advice

"I am not a big fan of the toilet because the group bonk possibilities are very limited. There is hardly enough space for three people. Seven of us did it once, but nobody could move; it was pointless."

## Pros & cons

+ You can use the toilet brush as a spank paddle (if clean).
+ You can blindfold your partner with toilet paper.
+ Spraying the toilet with the air freshener before bonking will give you an impression of bonking in a field of orange blossoms in spring or in a pine forest in autumn.
- The space and the design of the toilet stall will remind you of a cheap motel.
- The noise of a sick colleague next door could turn you off.
- The danger of being noticed leaving the women's/men's toilet.

## When to go there?

Avoid the hour after lunch (2-3 pm)

# PART 3: THE OFFICE BONKASUTRA

The 53 positions selected by our expert will let you discover a magical world where imagination, enthusiasm and sensuality meet: they will make you love your job.

Which positions work in different types of offices? How to fully exploit the furniture? How to enhance pleasure?

In the following pages you will discover that it is possible to do much better than the missionary on top of your office desk.

# THE BASICS

## The bonk creativity law

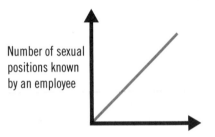

Number of sexual positions known by an employee

% of time spent by the employee watching porn at work

## Men/Woman balance law

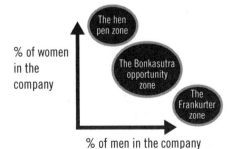

% of women in the company

The hen pen zone

The Bonkasutra opportunity zone

The Frankurter zone

% of men in the company

## The Pleasure Podium

### Expert Opinion

"This position especially suits computer geeks as it can give an impression of making love to your PC."

### Difficulty:

★★☆☆☆

## GMB (Good Morning Blowjob)

### Expert Opinion

"You will come to work happy and always on time. You risk a sharp increase in your productivity."

### Difficulty:

★☆☆☆☆

## The Classic

### Expert Opinion

"This is the position to use when you are doing it for the first time at work. It's a safe bet and never goes out of fashion. I have performed it over 500 times and can tell you that it works on all types of desks and with all types of colleagues."

### Difficulty:

## In Search of the Lost File

### Expert Opinion

"All colleagues wearing skirts love this position. If anyone enters, she can get dressed in a flash and pretend she was working. It may be somewhat more difficult for the gentlemen to do the same."

### Difficulty:

# The Pleasuring Heights

## Expert Opinion

"Have you noticed that about three-quarters of low cupboards in your company are at a perfect height for this position?"

### Difficulty:

★★★★☆

# The-King-of-the-Boardroom Table

## Expert Opinion

"For once you will not get bored at a meeting. You will even leave satisfied with your accomplishments."

### Difficulty:

★☆☆☆☆

## The e-Wheelbarrow

### Expert Opinion

"A convenient position when your colleague tells you she doesn't have time to bonk because she has an important document to prepare. Yes we can!"

### Difficulty:

## The Control Tower

### Expert Opinion

"If she is busy she can catch up on her e-mail with her feet."

### Difficulty:

# The Big Drum

## Expert Opinion

"Go for it with gusto and reveal your knack for drumming. Personally I clear the cupboard beforehand so as to augment the resonance."

## Difficulty:

★★★☆☆

# The Headstand of Delight

## Expert Opinion

"If she complains that her head hurts, slide the mouse pad under it as a cushion."

## Difficulty:

★★★☆☆

## The Love Nest

### Expert Opinion

"A great position for lovers, but remember to dust beforehand."

### Difficulty:

★★☆☆☆

## The Plug & Play

### Expert Opinion

"Use your hands to discover all the functions of your new keyboard. Experts will quickly locate the key shortcuts..."

### Difficulty:

★☆☆☆☆

# The Welcome Shag

## Expert Opinion

"This position is reserved for the shorter people, as the actions behind the reception desk of the tall ones among you might not go unnoticed. The very tall can give it a go, but on their knees."

## Difficulty:

★★★☆☆

# The Reverse Plug & Play

## Expert Opinion

"This is a variation of the Plug & Play position. Find the Plug & Play position, and then rotate 180°."

## Difficulty:

★★★★★

## The Love Waterfall

### Expert Opinion

"Be careful with the noises you make. The others might think that you are stuck inside and knocking on the door for help, and come to your rescue."

### Difficulty:

★★☆☆☆

## The Bermuda Triangle

### Expert Opinion

"The famous triangle inside of which all objects disappear…"

### Difficulty:

★★★☆☆

## The Six-Legged Dragon

### Expert Opinion

"A Chinese position to be executed on supplies that are stamped 'Made in China'."

### Difficulty:

★★☆☆☆

## The Brilliant Horse

### Expert Opinion

"Another good reason why you should demand a big computer screen from the IT personnel."

### Difficulty:

★★★☆☆

## The +

### Expert Opinion

"This is a difficult position. Be gentle or you risk falling backwards, transforming the + into an X..."

### Difficulty:

★★★★☆

## The Carpet Master

### Expert Opinion

"A good way of making it clear once and for all who is the boss in the department."

### Difficulty:

★☆☆☆☆

# The Bamboo Pirouette

## Expert Opinion

"This position will allow you to conveniently hide your partner behind your desk in case anyone enters, and make them think that you are just doing some push ups."

### Difficulty:

★★★★☆

# The Levitating Bamboo

## Expert Opinion

"You must learn the art of levitation. I suggest the method of the Tibetan Shamen, available on the internet."

### Difficulty:

★★★★★

## The Pie of Surprise

### Expert Opinion

"An alternative to The Classic for those who don't have their own office."

### Difficulty:

★☆☆☆☆

## The Sticky Scorpio

### Expert Opinion

"Gentlemen, don't stay in this position for more than five minutes or all the blood will gather in your head, which can cause erectile issues that your partner will not appreciate."

### Difficulty:

★★★★★

# The Download

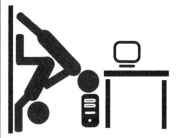

## Expert Opinion

"This is the most complex position of the Bonkasutra. Open the CD/DVD player of your computer and place a glass of water there to hydrate during your efforts."

## Difficulty:

# The Sloth

## Expert Opinion

"This is an ideal position for an open- plan office. Your colleagues will simply assume that you are away."

## Difficulty:

## The Love Seat

### Expert Opinion

"She will love her new chair..."

### Difficulty:

★★★☆☆

## The Sucker

### Expert Opinion

"The sweatier she will get, the easier it will be to accomplish this position."

### Difficulty:

★★★☆☆

# The New Toilet Seat

## Expert Opinion

"If you get hot, flush!"

## Difficulty:

★★★☆☆

# The Bridge of Sighs

## Expert Opinion

"If you are very discreet you can do it under the table of a colleague while he's working."

## Difficulty:

★☆☆☆☆

# The Magic Mail Cart

## Expert Opinion

"A good way of saying 'good morning' to all your colleagues."

### Difficulty:

★★★☆☆

# North and South Poles

## Expert Opinion

"Most adapted cupboards can be found in the archives. Calm space, but quite often frequented by colleagues who want to bonk. Remember to book in advance."

### Difficulty:

★★★☆☆

# The Evaluation Meeting

## Expert Opinion

"The only real way of advancing at work."

## Difficulty:

# The Pleasure Closet

## Expert Opinion

"If anyone enters, close the door quickly and put away your equipment."

## Difficulty:

## The Enchanted Copy Machine

### Expert Opinion

"Press the 'copy' button regularly to make souvenirs of these pleasant work moments."

### Difficulty:

## The Y of the Chinese Circus

### Expert Opinion

"I saw a couple perform this in China, and the girl twirled plates on a pencil at the same time."

### Difficulty:

# The Golden Gate Bridge

## Expert Opinion

"A good way for different departments to bond."

## Difficulty:

★★☆☆☆

# The Neon of Venus

## Expert Opinion

"Be careful, some might think you are trying to steal the neon lights in your building."

## Difficulty:

★★★★☆

# The Open-Space Chant

## Expert Opinion

"A good way of sharing your sense of rhythm with the entire company."

## Difficulty:

# The Mutual Appreciation

## Expert Opinion

"A nice way of putting the equality of men and women in a workplace into practice."

## Difficulty:

# The Burning Rock

## Expert Opinion

"Place your partner on the radiator for a few minutes and you can skip the foreplay."

### Difficulty:

★★☆☆☆

# The Devilish Coat Rack

## Expert Opinion

"A position that will remind her of the monkey bars of her youth."

### Difficulty:

★★★★☆

# The Scooter

## Expert Opinion

"I have often tried this one but never succeeded. If you accomplish it, do send me your advice and photographs."

## Difficulty:

★★★★★

# The Team Building

## Expert Opinion

"A team-building exercise that is free and can be performed anywhere with everyone in all companies."

## Difficulty:

★★★☆☆

# The Rocket Launch

## Expert Opinion

"A position that is particularly convenient for a long-sighted colleague who likes to look at the computer screen from a short distance."

## Difficulty:

★★☆☆☆

# The Interior Designer

## Expert Opinion

"Incline your desk to enjoy a new perspective and get new ideas."

## Difficulty:

★★☆☆☆

## The Paper Stack Cushion

### Expert Opinion

"If she makes too much noise, place her head in a box with printing paper that will suppress her sounds."

### Difficulty:

★★☆☆☆

## The Secret Drawer

### Expert Opinion

"Suggest she puts her hands on the chewing gum stuck underneath the desk for a better grip."

### Difficulty:

★★★☆☆

# The Pleasure Hideaway

## Expert Opinion

"Don't try to work while you are being pleasured or you risk sending your boss an e-mail which could go something like this: 'Dear boss, I would like you to swallow the big folder and lick the pages'."

### Difficulty:

★☆☆☆☆

# Superman's Cape

## Expert Opinion

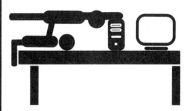

"I worked with Superman before he switched to his current career. It was him who showed me this position. But it was me who advised him to use his cape to hide his partner if someone was approaching."

### Difficulty:

★★★☆☆

# The e-Bats

## Expert Opinion

"I performed this position three times. The first time we fell on the monitor and the second time we crushed the printer. The third time it went well at first, but then we had to call a colleague..."

## Difficulty:

★★★★★

# The Reverse

## Expert Opinion

"With a bit of luck, you may go unnoticed if someone enters while you are in this position. If they do see you, just tell them you are looking for a pencil."

## Difficulty:

★★★★☆

# The Very High Mountain

## Expert Opinion

"This is one of my favourite positions. I installed secret handles on top of all my office cupboards so that my colleagues can get a firm grip."

## Difficulty:

# PART 4: POSSIBLE DANGERS DURING A BONK AT WORK

What are the risks you are exposed to during a bonk at work?
What to do when you are caught in the act?
How to master bonking in the toilet?

In the following pages you will find out that, yes, you can get away with it when your boss walks in on you with your trousers around your ankles!

# THE BASICS

## The Bill Law

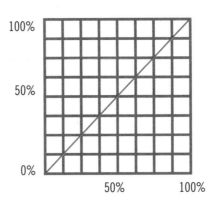

Probability of getting caught

100%

50%

0%

50%    100%

Time spent bonking at work

## Expert Opinion

"If you spend 100% of your time bonking at work, you have a 100% chance of getting caught. It's as simple as that."

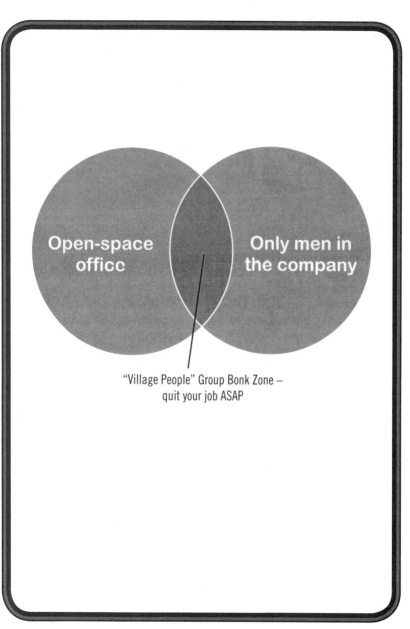

Open-space officc

Only men in the company

"Village People" Group Bonk Zone – quit your job ASAP

## PROBLEM: Your partner faints

You are in your office with a colleague, making your overtures for a bonk. Your colleague's eyes suddenly look glassy, he/she is about to faint…

## SOLUTION: "It wasn't me"

1. Make sure your partner isn't dead.
2. When nobody is in the hallway, grab your partner by the feet and drag to the hallway.
3. Once in the hallway, make sure to drag partner far enough from your office.
4. Return to your office, get dressed and don't worry, sooner or later a colleague will find him/her.

## Expert Opinion

"Leaving your colleague in the corridor could expose you to resentment once he/she wakes up… I would suggest you put him/her in a corner of your office and wait till he/she awakens.

"Lay your colleague down on the floor, and tape pieces of paper on the body. That way, if a colleague happens to walk in, you can tell him that you are preparing a big file."

## Testimonial

"My partner was a bit on the heavy side. I had to roll her out of the office like a big tree trunk. Quick and easy!" Fred, Systems Analyst, Edinburgh

## PROBLEM: You feel like you might faint

You are in the middle of your saucy break when suddenly you feel weak and might faint.

## SOLUTION: Fido's collar

1. Don't faint. If your partner has read this book, you'll find yourself naked in the hallway.
   The reason for your dizzy turn is the fact that your blood is concentrated in your genitals and not enough is left for your brain.
2. Grab your computer mouse.
3. Use its cord to fashion a tourniquet around your neck to stop the blood from draining from your brain and rushing down to your genitals.
4. Finish what you started with the colleague, with your mouse cord wrapped around your neck.
5. Get dressed and return to your desk. Don't forget to remove the mouse from around your neck (especially important if you are on your way to a meeting).

## Expert Opinion

"If you can find another mouse with a cord, you could even suggest a little bondage to your colleague... Why not spice things up a bit!"

## Testimonial

"I have a laptop and don't use a mouse. I wanted to use my sticky tape to make my tourniquet, but a big chunk of tape got stuck on the desk and it removed my pubic hair. Ouch!" Jay, Production Controller, Bath

## PROBLEM: Your boss comes

You are in the middle of romping about in your office with your department's secretary. Just as things are taking off, your boss enters.

## SOLUTION: The green-eyed monster

1. When you spot your boss, stop all movement.
2. Hold yourself upright and stay proud (your boss would surely love to be in your place).
3. Say without fear: "Hello boss, how are you? I took the liberty of bonking your secretary."
4. Seeing his bewilderment, simply add: "We are roughly halfway through."
5. If he's still there, say indignantly: "How long will you be ogling us like this? Bloody pervert!"
6. This should get him out of the room. You can now resume your movements progressively.

## Expert Opinion

"A recent study shows that 37% of bosses dream of bonking their secretary. I therefore assume that 63% of the secretaries are ugly."

## Testimonial

"My boss sat on the corner of the desk and said: 'I'll wait. I urgently need her to help me with a file.'" Simon, Broker, Truro

## PROBLEM: You receive an important phone call

 You are in the middle of bonking a colleague when your phone rings. You must answer this urgent call, but you really don't want to stop mid-bonk.

## SOLUTION: "It's not me, it's you"

1. Answer your phone and continue bonking.
2. Listen to your caller's request.
3. He will hear that you are bonking. Take charge and reverse the situation by saying: "What's that noise? Are you bonking someone? Are you bonking in the middle of the day in the office?!"
4. He will deny this outright. Say to him: "Well, you're obviously lying. I am completely appalled and disappointed; I thought we'd established a good relationship. I can't believe that you are calling me while bonking God knows who; it's repulsive! Call me back when you have finished, you exhibitionist."
5. Finish your bonk at your own time; he won't call you any time soon.

## Expert Opinion

"You can explain the bonk noises by saying that your financial director has rented your office to a porn film production company to save your company from bankruptcy, and that five actors are hard at work at that very moment less than 1.8 m (6 ft) away from you."

## Testimonial

"I had a client who made my life miserable for three years. One day I recorded our phone conversation and added shag noises. I then sent it as an MP3 to everyone in my company, entitled 'Mr Smith shagging at work yesterday!' Now every time he comes for a meeting, everyone looks at him with contempt, and he doesn't understand why." Gina, Banker, Slough

You are gripped with desire and start bonking a colleague even though you know your next appointment is about to arrive. He arrives, waits for 15 minutes, but you still haven't finished. The thought of inviting him in for a threesome crosses your mind, but he might not take it well.

## SOLUTION: The desk of hidden desires

1. Even though you have not finished, stop bonking.
2. Go and get your next appointment.
3. Sit him opposite you. You must now find a way to clear your head of sex thoughts that are stopping you from thinking and working normally.
4. While he is talking, carefully open your zip.
5. Whack off under the desk without making it known to your visitor.
6. Be mindful not to make a funny face at the crucial moment.
7. Once finished, zip up your trousers or skirt and continue your meeting.
8. Be kind – don't shake hands when he leaves.

## Expert Opinion

"When confronted by such a situation, I ask my bonk partner to crawl under the desk while I go to get my next appointment..."

## Testimonial

"I was so turned on that I even found the fat 55-year-old man I was meeting really sexy." Laura, Insurance Assesor, Tring

## PROBLEM: You have an erection while making a presentation

You are giving a presentation when suddenly you have an enormous erection. It's impossible to bring it down, and your entire audience will surely notice it and mock you.

## SOLUTION: A very big boat

1. Don't panic. Nobody actually listens to presentations so it's probable that nobody has noticed it yet.
2. Pre-empt any comments and say: "Incidentally, if anyone has noticed a big bump in my trousers, be reassured, it's not my penis. It's just an enormous key-ring in the shape of the Titanic that my wife gave me for my birthday."
3. Your colleagues will wish you a happy birthday and won't pay any attention to your erection.

## Expert Opinion

"When I'm in such a situation, I think of our Key Accounts Manager. It's radical: she is so ugly that the zeppelin is down in less than two seconds."

## Testimonial

"The room was dark and they couldn't see me very well. I took advantage of it and used my penis as a pointing device, much like in a Chinese shadow puppet theatre." David, Telecoms, Birmingham

## PROBLEM: Your partner is making too much noise

**Oh yes!**
**Oh my God!**
**OH MY GOD!**

You are bonking your colleague in your office. She is making really bizarre noises and your colleagues might pop in at any moment to see what's going on. You have told her several times to bring the volume down, but nothing works. You are a master bonker; she just can't stop screaming.

## SOLUTION: The new soundproofer

1. Bonk away while inching closer to your rubbish bin.
2. Place the bin on your partner's head. The bin and all the paper in it will serve as a very efficient soundproofing device.
3. Continue bonking.
4. Don't take the bin off her head until you finish. And don't be afraid that your colleague will be angry – this was probably not the first time she's had this problem and surely not the last. She will be grateful that you've found a practical solution to her problem.

## Expert Opinion

"I use this method because my partners often scream: 'Oh Stanley! Ohhh Stanley!' Talk about being given away in less than two minutes."

## Testimonial

"I soundproofed with egg cartons. My colleagues think that I am fond of eggs and bring them to me when they spend weekends in the country." Jo, Sales, Hull

## PROBLEM: You are making too much noise while bonking at work

**Oh!
Oh!
Yes!**

You are bonking your super-hot colleague. You are so excited that you can't contain your moans. If this continues, the entire department will soon be in your office wondering why you are making so much noise.

## SOLUTION: The avatar

1. Be careful, your partner might put a rubbish bin on *your* head.
2. Continue bonking and open the Intranet.
3. Look at the company mug shot of the colleague you are bonking. (All employees have a bad photo of them on the Intranet.) If this doesn't work, look at the profiles of the accounts personnel...
4. Go back to bonking and, as soon as you feel yourself taking off a bit too much, look again the photograph that calmed you down.

## Expert Opinion

"My technique in such situations is to open a big spreadsheet full of numbers. This calms me down immediately. Did you know that an MIT study has shown that Excel is one of 100 factors that caused a drop in fertility rates in developed countries? Employees who use it more than seven hours a day don't have enough libido in the evenings to make love to their spouses."

## Testimonial

"When I make too much noise shagging I put the entire computer mouse into my mouth. It works pretty well! Well, if you don't mind the cable dangling from your mouth." Samantha, Designer, Auckland

## PROBLEM: You are caught photocopying...

You decide to kill some time by photocopying your bum. But the moment you press "copy", a colleague walks in and sees you sitting naked on the photocopier.

## SOLUTION: The test

1. Don't panic. Stay on the copy machine and wait until the copying is finished.
2. Then jump off and start putting your trousers back on, and say: "It's really strange, this new campaign against colon cancer that the company has started. We all have to make photocopies of our bums and take them to the company doctor to examine!"
3. Your colleague will be astounded.
4. Ask if he/she has done it. The answer is invariably "No".
5. Explain that everyone has to do it by this evening. Suggest that he/she gets on with it and you'll kindly take it straight to the doctor.

## Expert Opinion

"Don't overdo it when copying your bum, especially if you are a man: a study has shown that this practice considerably lowers fertility rates. In fact, the light from the copy machine blinds the spermatozoids for several days, which means that they can't find their target when they are shot into action."

## Testimonial

"I got all the girls in the company to photocopy their breasts by telling them it was for breast cancer screening." Gilles, Sales Admin, Lille

## PROBLEM: You make a banging noise while bonking at work

You are happily bonking a colleague, but your movements are making a drumming noise. Your boss is in an office nearby and might be intrigued by the noise and walk into your office to discover that there is no musical performance but a spectacle of a different kind.

## SOLUTION: The magic bubbles

1. Stop bonking and get dressed.
2. Go to the mailroom and get several metres of bubble wrap.
3. Come back to the office.
4. Undress and wrap yourself up in the bubble wrap.
5. Ask your bonk colleague to take a pair of scissors and make a little hole in the middle in order to... well, you know.
6. Bonk her while wrapped in the bubble wrap. This will considerably diminish the banging noises.

## Expert Opinion

"Bubble wrap can also help you in attempting some of the more perilous positions of the Bonkasutra since it will protect you in case of falling. Mind you, I never use this technique because my very energetic hip movements tear the bubble wrap apart with each move."

## Testimonial

"I used this method. I looked like a giant spring roll." Tim, Buyer, Telford

## PROBLEM: You are caught watching a porn website

You haven't bonked any colleagues in two months and you are therefore highly depressed. While looking for solace on pornographic websites, a colleague walks in and catches you looking at some rather explicit images.

## SOLUTION: The after work hobby

1. Don't panic when your colleague catches you.
2. Tell her to come closer to help you. She might not understand why you need help looking at porn sites.
3. Explain that your boss has a second job: he is a porn star on the web. Tell her that you are trying to find one of his videos.
4. Your colleague will now look at the porn website with you.

## Expert Opinion

"Don't try to re-enact everything you see in X-rated films. You can't just expect to dress like a pizza delivery boy and tell your colleague: "Hello, it's your pizza delivery!" to incite a wild bonk."

## Testimonial

"After being caught looking at a porn website, the rumour that the boss was a porn star spread like wildfire. My colleagues launched a massive hunt for my 'porn star' boss in one of over 14,000 videos on the website I was caught on."
Steve, Accountant, London

## PROBLEM: You are caught with an inflatable doll in your office

It's now been three months since you've bonked a colleague, and even the porn sites are no longer helpful. You buy an inflatable doll, but a colleague walks in while you are inflating it.

## SOLUTION: Crocodile Dundee

1. Don't show any sign of panic when your colleague surprises you.
2. Put on a weary look.
3. Tell your colleague: "I'm disgusted: I ordered an inflatable crocodile for my kids on a Chinese website for 65p, and they sent me an inflatable doll!"
4. Add: "I was just blowing up my crocodile to check it out because with this big hole in the middle I thought it was punctured."
5. Ask: "Do you think I could give this to the boss as a Secret Santa?"

## Expert Opinion

"I was a bit drunk on holidays once and I tried to bonk an inflatable beach crocodile! I confused it with my girlfriend at the time who often wore imitation crocodile trousers."

## Testimonial

"Such delivery confusion actually happened to me. I couldn't be bothered to exchange it and my kids aged 4 and 6 played with an inflatable doll on the beach all summer." Owen, CSR, Liverpool

## PROBLEM: You are bonking in the toilet and people can see two pairs of shoes

You are both in a toilet cubicle in order to bonk but there is a big gap at the base. Your colleagues entering the toilet will see two pairs of feet in one stall and immediately know what's going on.

## SOLUTION: The young and the restless

1. When you hear someone entering the toilet, imitate your boss's voice.
2. Whisper to your colleague, telling her to imitate the voice of a colleague who nobody likes. Let's call her Miriam.
3. Imitating your boss's voice, say loudly: "Oh yes Miriam, you are a hot piece of ass! If you'll keep going like this you will get your big promotion!"
4. Your colleague should answer: "Oh yes, take me, you crazy boss you!"
5. Wait happily at your desk for the rumour of the boss's liaison to start.
6. Look very surprised when you hear that the boss is bonking Miriam.
7. Start spreading the rumour as well.

## Expert Opinion

"Give one of your shoes to your colleague and bonk while each is standing on one foot. Be careful not to drop her into the toilet."

## Testimonial

"A year ago my colleague and I read the book *How to Poo at Work*, which mentions the problem of doors with bottom openings. We have since been shagging while levitating one metre up." Jules, Freight Agent, Norwich

## PROBLEM: You bonk in the toilet and your boss knocks on the door

You are in the toilet preparing to bonk. The door a gap at the bottom, making your feet visible. You have just started when your boss knocks on your door. You have no idea how to explain what you are really doing in the toilet.

## SOLUTION: Protect the fort

1. Don't say anything. He doesn't know who is in the toilet.
2. Take the toilet brush.
3. Dip it in the toilet.
4. Throw it out over the door and try to drop it on your boss's head.
5. He will leave surprised and annoyed.

## Expert Opinion

"Another possibility: imitate the voice of a colleague and say: 'Yes, it's taken, this is Denis, and I have diarrhoea. Please leave me alone!'"

## Testimonial

"Even after I threw the toilet brush he wouldn't leave and kept knocking. I threw a wet toilet roll and the toilet seat out too. He finally left after that."
Juliet, Staff Writer, Coventry

## PROBLEM: You break the toilet door while bonking

You bonked so hard in the toilet that you broke the door. If you don't do anything your boss or the financial director might start an investigation to find out who in the company breaks toilet doors. It could very well lead them to you.

## SOLUTION: The jigsaw puzzle gift

1. Together with your partner, gather all the pieces of the broken door.
2. Leave the toilet and be careful not to be caught with pieces of the door in your hands.
3. Place all the pieces on the desk of a colleague who has left his desk and put big pieces of sticky tape over them, making it seem like he was trying to repair it.
4. All your colleagues who pass in front of his office will think that it was him who broke the toilet door.

## Expert Opinion

"Since 2009, and after many accidents of this nature, an EU directive finally obliges toilet-door producers to make doors that can resist lateral pressure of 250 kg (550 lbs)."

## Testimonial

"My boss entered the moment the door broke..." Piers, Director, Frome

## PROBLEM: You flushed the toilet seven times

You bonked a colleague in the toilet, on the seat. While you were bonking, she inadvertently flushed the toilet seven times. All your colleagues who are in the toilet will think that someone is very sick and will try to find out who it is. They could very well think it's you.

## SOLUTION: Breaking news

1. After your bonk return discreetly to your post.
2. Go to one of your colleagues and ask if he's seen the boss. Tell him you are worried for her.
3. Add: "I heard her flush seven times earlier in the toilet; she must be having diarrhoea from hell, poor thing."
4. Continue spreading the boss-has-diarrhoea rumour.

## Expert Opinion

"10 litres (2 gallons) of water, seven times. Now that is not a very environmentally responsible bonk. Not good, not good at all."

## Testimonial

"To make the story more credible, I slipped into the boss' office and sprayed perfume all over it. That way all employees who came to her office could smell it, which proved that she spent a lot of time in the toilet." Jane, Admin, Ipswich

## PROBLEM: You put a foot in the toilet while bonking

You were bonking in the toilet and, while trying a new position, put your foot on the toilet seat but it slipped and now your shoe is completely wet. You will be embarrassed all day at work with your wet shoe.

## SOLUTION: Too hot

1. When you finish, put your other foot in the toilet too.
2. Leave the toilet with your wet feet.
3. Go and see your boss.
4. Tell him: "Could we set the air conditioning a bit lower? I am really hot; my feet are sweating – look!"
5. Tell the same thing to all the colleagues you come across.

## Expert Opinion

"You really have to be a beginner if you don't remember to shut the toilet seat before bonking. The level of workplace bonking these days sometimes really depresses me."

## Testimonial

"My foot got stuck. My colleague had to call a plumber. I've been living in hell ever since. My colleagues call me 'Sh*t Foot'". Ben, Producer, Leeds

## PROBLEM: You break your partner's arm

 You got a bit carried away during your last work bonk and accidentally broke your partner's arm. The reasonable option would be to take him/her to the doctor, but you don't know how you could explain the circumstances.

## SOLUTION: DIY

1. Grab a big bundle of paper from the paper shredder.
2. Take it to the toilet and fill one of the sinks with water. Put the shredded paper in the water and wait till it soaks in (if you haven't got a sink nearby, chew the shreds of paper one by one to moisten them).
3. Take the wet paper back to your office. Sit your colleague on your chair and place the keyboard under the broken arm (to be used as splint).
4. Wrap the wet paper around the arm. You are making a cast.
5. Tell your colleague to go to the toilet and place the wrapped arm under the drying fan for the cast to dry.
6. Finally, use the mouse wire to make a sling.

## Expert Opinion

"I don't understand: how exactly did you manage to break the arm? Maybe you should drink a little less coffee; it seems to be agitating you a tad too much."

## Testimonial

"The next day I wrote on his cast: 'Sorry for breaking your arm because you didn't deliver your on time; it was stupid on my part. Fiona'. Fiona is a colleague I really can't stand." Giles, Revenue Agent, Sydney

# PART 5: POTENTIAL POST-BONK PROBLEMS

Which dangers lurk out there once we finish bonking?
How do you handle yourself when you commit bonk errors and how do you undo the damage to your image?
How do you face the unpleasant bonk-related rumours about you?

Find out on the following pages that your career isn't necessarily over if a sex tape of your bonk is circulating the entire company and beyond.

# THE BASICS

## The Blue Law

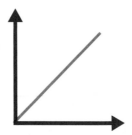

Number of porn sites you watch at work

Number of viagra spam e-mails you recieve on your professional e-mail

## The Danger Law

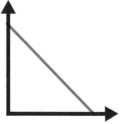

Number of colleagues who think you are nice

Number of colleagues saying you have bonked at work

## PROBLEM: You left your underwear in the toilet

You bonked a colleague in the toilet, but when leaving you left your underwear behind. A colleague found it and sent around an e-mail telling everyone that whoever left their underwear in the toilet can get it back from them. If they find out it was yours, your colleagues will never stop mocking you and call you "Mr/Mrs Pants" for at least a year.

## SOLUTION: The good friend

1. Go see the colleague who sent the e-mail.
2. Tell him that they are Gerry's boxers/Geraldine's knickers but that he/she was too embarrassed to come and get them. You came instead of him/her.
3. Go to Gerry's/Geraldine's desk and say: "Hiya, here is your underwear. You left it in the toilet."
4. He/she will try denying it, but it's too late; the damage is done.

## Expert Opinion

"Use the PSTSS technique that I invented. It stands for Pants, Socks, Trousers, Shirt, Shoes. This is a strong mnemonic tool to help you get dressed quickly after a work bonk without making mistakes because of time constraints."

## Testimonial

"When I brought 'his' boxers over, my colleague wasn't at his post. I carefully folded them and placed them on his keyboard, with a post-it saying: "Gerry, here are your pants. You left them in the toilet." Matt, Facilitator, Yeovil

## PROBLEM: You come back with a post-bonk glow

You have just secretly bonked a colleague in the middle of the afternoon. You come back to your post with a glowing red face, which makes it pretty clear to your colleagues what you have just done.

## SOLUTION: High Definition

1. Approach your colleagues to spark the questioning.
2. Wait for someone to ask: "What's up with you? You're all red!"
3. To which you respond: "I know! It's my new screen. It's got a 1:1,000,000,000 contrast and it works a bit too well; I'm all burnt!"
4. To reinforce your statement, put your sunglasses on as you start leaving and say: "Well, I have to go back. Wish me luck..."
5. Go back to work.

## Expert Opinion

"Everyone has a couple of colleagues who say they go running or to the gym during the lunch break, and come back red in the face and all sweaty. Open your eyes: they always leave in twos, and they are the opposite sex. You can be sure that more than half of them go bonking in the park or in the woods behind the building!"

## Testimonial

"When I saw I was completely red in the face, I tightened the knot of my tie to make it seem like that caused the change in colour. However, I had forgotten to zip up my trousers..." Martin, Statistician, Cambridge

## PROBLEM: You are stuck overnight and have nothing to talk about

You end a long day of work with a quick bonk in the meeting room with a colleague. When you want to leave you realize that the door is locked. You will have to spend the night together, but you have absolutely no desire to talk to them.

## SOLUTION: A long-term relationship

1. Try one more time to open the door.
2. If it still doesn't open, make yourself comfortable on a table and wait for him/her to start talking to you.
3. He/she will most probably start with the famous question: "Was it good for you?"
4. Answer: "Yes." Then turn around and start snoring.

## Expert Opinion

"McGyver would cut the door with a laser beam from the video projector. Follow his example!"

## Testimonial

"We called the locksmith. The 'emergency service' has cost me $1,600 that I am still paying off." Michel, Computer Programmer, Toronto

## PROBLEM: You are accused of booking the meeting room too often

The meeting room has become your bonk place of choice, and you visit it often. A bit too often, perhaps, as some people are starting to complain that they can't book meetings anymore since you're always in there.

## SOLUTION: Jealousy

1. Don't say why you need the meeting room so often.
2. Ask whoever is accusing you of hogging the meeting room: "A bit jealous, are we? Not enough meetings on your schedule?"
3. This will make your colleague ill at ease and wonder if he/she hasn't been looking sufficiently busy and important.
4. Leave him/her with: "You'll get invited when you're more intelligent."
5. Continue to book the meeting room three times a day.

## Expert Opinion

"Spice up your sex life: bonk in the meeting room without booking it!"

## Testimonial

"I've shared the tips on meeting room shagging with a colleague and she started doing it too. We now book the room so often we sometimes have to shag there at the same time." Sarah, Architect, Kettering

## PROBLEM: You have a huge lovebite

 You've just bonked a colleague. While getting dressed you notice that you have an enormous lovebite on your neck. You can't hide it with your hand all day, especially if this happens early in the morning.

## SOLUTION: A new trend

1. Go back to your post like nothing happened.
2. The annoying colleague (there's always one in every company) will make a comment about your lovebite.
3. You should answer: "Of course I have a lovebite; it's the international Day of the Lovebite!"
4. Then add: "The boss gave it to me; he is totally into the concept."
5. Finally suggest to her: "Go and ask him to give you one too."
6. Watch as your colleague makes her way to the boss's office.

## Expert Opinion

"Don't forget that on 12 June this year we will be celebrating the first international Bonk at Work Day! Many thanks to the Bill Clinton Foundation which lobbied vigorously for this day within the United Nations."

## Testimonial

"I tried to make everyone think that the hickey was actually a consequence of a rare illness originating in Africa. I thought this would make me seem adventurous in the eyes of my colleagues, but now everyone is avoiding me because they fear it's contagious." Dean, Auditor, Milton Keynes

## PROBLEM: You fall asleep naked

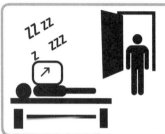 You bonked a colleague and it was intense. So intense that you fell asleep afterwards, exhausted. You don't wake up until another colleague walks into your office and discovers you naked.

## SOLUTION: The Yogi

1. Stand up and carry yourself with confidence.
2. Don't try to cover yourself up at all, even if you are uncomfortable.
3. Tell your colleague: "Yes, I am naked. You interrupted me in the middle of my session of naked yoga. You can leave now."
4. Your colleague will look at you strangely.
5. Take a seat behind your desk and say: "Didn't you hear me?"
6. Be consistent and stay naked all day in your office, and even go to all your meetings naked.

## Expert Opinion

"A company in Scandinavia had 'Naked Fridays'. According to its HR department this has made the team more cohesive. In meetings, all participants are naked. If this happened in Italy, it would quickly turn into an orgy."

## Testimonial

"When my colleague entered, I immediately took up a meditating position, like a naked Buddha. She thought that was sweet, took off her clothes and joined me. She relaxed so much that I bonked her." Pablo, Travel Agent, Staines

## PROBLEM: You are caught calling sex hotlines

You call sex hotlines to enliven your work. A few weeks later the Financial Director summons you to his office and waves your phone records in front of you, with the sex hotline number marked in bright yellow marker.

## SOLUTION: A Personal Call

1. Your Financial Director will ask you: "Could you tell me what are all these calls about?" Get up, look annoyed and head towards your most timid colleague. Let's call him Dennis.
2. Yell at him: "Dennis, you've got to be kidding, you called the sex hotline again from my desk! I'm sick of it!"
3. Add: "I've already told you to get some treatment for your sexual urges."
4. Then say to the Financial Director: "Please forgive him. With his bad breath nobody will go near him and he thinks the hotline operator is in love with him."

## Expert Opinion

"I've calculated that an hour on a sex hotline is three times less expensive than an hour with the company psychologist who is supposed to help the employees cope better with their work. I can send you this calculation so you can give it to your Financial Director and propose significant savings for the company."

## Testimonial

"I was caught on the hop and told them that it wasn't my fault – I sincerely thought that Ursula *was* the new company therapist." John, Telecoms, Rutland

## PROBLEM: You don't want to see them again

You bonked a colleague. Since then she has been asking you out for drinks or wanting to talk about what happened. You, however, don't want to see her again and just want her to leave you alone.

## SOLUTION: Networking

1. See the clingy colleague at her desk.
2. Ask: "Can you do me a favour?"
3. Happy that you are finally paying attention to her, she will eagerly say "Yes".
4. Say: "Can you fix me up with your mate? I realized that she is the only one I haven't bonked in the company and she's missing in my bonk stats database."
5. Said colleague will leave you alone from now on.

## Expert Opinion

"If you feel confident, propose a threesome! You, the needy colleague and her mate in the meeting room."

## Testimonial

"She slapped me, so I spread a rumour that she's into exhibitionist S&M. Four other colleagues are now more interested in her." Sam, Advertising, Sale

## PROBLEM: You are caught on security camera

You bonked your colleague unnoticed... or so you thought. The next morning the security guard calls you over and shows you the video of your bonk. You can't deny it – you are perfectly recognizable.

## SOLUTION: A new business opportunity

1. Ask the security guard if he has the entire bonk on film.
2. Offer him a deal: you will sell the video to a porn film production company and he will get a share of the proceeds. (80% for you, 20% for the security guy and 0% for your partner who has no idea that he/she is about to become a porn star.)
3. Take the video and sell it as "Extreme Work Bonking".
4. With the proceeds you can create your own X-rated film company, with the security guard as film editor and you as the artistic director.

## Expert Opinion

"This is excellent proof that one can improve one's work situation by bonking. What do you enjoy more, shagging or making spreadsheets until 10 pm?"

## Testimonial

"I showed the video to a professional in the field. He didn't want to buy it, but he gave me some tips and now I bonk like a pro!" Russell, Designer, Chingford

## PROBLEM: You find out you have an STI

Your annual medical exam reveals that you have caught a sexually transmitted infection. You have bonked a large porportion of your colleagues of the opposite sex and fear that you have spread it all over the company. It would be advisable to alert your partners of your condition, but you can't.

## SOLUTION: The newsletter

1. Never unveil that you have an STI. You would forever be treated like a radioactive plague carrier.
2. Find the computer of a colleague who isn't there and send this e-mail to everyone in the company: "Dear colleagues, I have caught a very contagious virus that can be transferred with handshakes. I apologize to everyone whom I have infected."
3. Don't forget to sign the e-mail with your colleague's name, for example Paul.
4. Complain about Paul to all your colleagues who you bonked and probably infected.

## Expert Opinion

"One of my colleagues once caught a rare STI. It made his member triple in size and change colour. I am not joking; in the end he couldn't even sit down!"

## Testimonial

"I sent the email from my boss' computer. Nobody wants to shake his hand anymore! He will soon resign and I will take his place." Jim, Sales, Vancouver

## PROBLEM: The porn film you made with your webcam is circulating everywhere

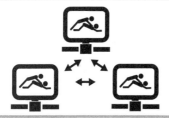 You filmed yourself with the webcam of your PC during a bonk. Since you are better at bonking than you are at IT, you mistakenly saved the film on the company server. Everybody has seen it and is looking at you funny. You must react.

## SOLUTION: The conference

1. Don't cry and whine to every colleague to please stop sending it around. It won't work.
2. Summon everyone to the meeting room. Say it's urgent.
3. Play the sex tape for them and explain each position to them with the help of a PowerPoint presentation that you must prepare beforehand.
4. When you finish, ask them: "OK, any questions? None? Fine then, we can all go back to work now. Thank you for your attention."This will give you a strong reputation in the company; everyone will stop laughing and your colleagues will probably see you as their hero who bonks at work and gets away with it.

## Expert Opinion

"If you feel like you have really captivated your audience, tell them you will now demonstrate different techniques of workplace bonking with a volunteer from the audience."

## Testimonial

"My colleagues now call me Mr. Sexxxx!" Adrian, Researcher, Leamington Spa

## PROBLEM: They call you El Bonko

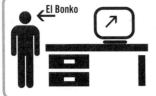

You have been bonking a lot at work recently and were caught more than once by your colleagues who now call you El Bonko. Asking them to stop would, without question, only incite them further.

## SOLUTION: Derivatives

You have to make it ridiculous for your colleagues to talk about it. To achieve that, assume your nickname 200%.

1. Have a T-shirt made that says, "El Bonko – Sex Instructor" and wear it every day at work.
2. Create an automatic signature for your e-mails: "El Bonko – All services and all positions – Available 24/7".
3. If you have a friend who is an avid computer programmer, get him to write a little programme "Customize your El Bonko" and e-mail it to your colleagues.
4. Offer coaching to your colleagues. They can bonk in front of a webcam while you provide live feedback.
5. After a few days, your colleagues will be sick of it and feel it's ridiculous to call you El Bonko.

## Expert Opinion

"Personally, I would enjoy being called El Bonko. After all, I have more than earned it!"

## Testimonial

"Everybody at my company loved my El Bonko – Sex Instructor T-shirt from day one. I created my clothing line under the brand of Mr Shag and I sell it on eBay. I earn more than I did before!" Edwin, Wolverhampton

## PROBLEM: You broke everything in your office

A bonk got out of hand and you broke everything in your office. You don't feel it's appropriate to ask your boss or your colleagues to help you put everything back into place.

## SOLUTION: SOS

1. Use your mobile phone to take pictures of the situation.
2. Sit behind your computer (if it's still in one piece) and start writing an e-mail to the HR department. Subject: "My boss wants to kill me."
3. Explain in the e-mail that you were attacked by your boss because you turned in your assignment one minute too late.
4. Attach the photos as proof.
5. Add that he may have been under the influence of alcohol or drugs, which will help you during an eventual lawsuit when he will say that it wasn't him or that he doesn't remember.
6. Wait patiently for your boss to be ordered to pay the damages or be fired.

## Expert Opinion

"For anyone who might be interested, I give courses of Feng Shui for Bonkers. The course teaches you how to organize your office to make it an ergonomic space with no risks, and how to adapt it to the teachings of the Bonkasutra."

## Testimonial

"I stayed late and replaced all the furniture in my office with the furniture of my colleague next door. When he came in the next morning he was asking if there had been an earthquake." René, VP of Marketing, Seattle

## PROBLEM: You are covered in massage oil

You spiced up your bonk with the help of sensual massage oil. Once finished, you stink of patchouli oil. It is impossible to return to work as usual.

## SOLUTION: The canine-feline technique

1. Tamper with the fire extinguisher.
2. Shower yourself with fire extinguisher foam. International standards require that the fire extinguisher contain a strong degreasing agent, so it will remove the oil from your skin.
3. Once you are completely covered in fire extinguishing foam, roll yourself on the carpet like a wet dog. The carpet will help you remove the remaining oil and of course the extinguisher foam.
4. Clean your back and other inaccessible parts of your body like a cat, by writhing along the walls and the legs of your desk.
5. Get dressed and go back to work.
6. Once you are home, take care of your skin and take at least five showers.

## Expert Opinion

"If you try to get dressed while covered in oil, your clothes will stick and get all greasy. You will resemble an otter rather than a dynamic employee."

## Testimonial

"I bonked a colleague who was really into organic products. He covered me in virgin olive oil – I felt like a bruschetta all day." Desirée, Stock Clerk, Wigan

## PROBLEM: You stained your clothes

You were clumsy during a bonk and stained your clothes. The white stain is particularly visible and impossible to remove.

## SOLUTION: The snow leopard

1. Don't go to the toilet to wash the stain off because a colleague who might walk in while you're drying off could think that you are drying your private parts.
2. Hide the stain with your hands and buy a pot of yoghurt from the canteen.
3. Use it to make several stains on your clothes to give them a snow leopard print if they are white, or the always fashionable leopard print if they are brown.
4. Enjoy the rest of your day sporting your stylish leopard-print clothes.

## Expert Opinion

"A nice adaptation of the leopard's fur method from the book *How to Poo at Work*, which, as you know, is a technique of safely leaving the toilet when we have stained the clothes there."

## Testimonial

"I made a zebra pattern with the correction fluid!" Maggie, Payroll Clerk, Deal

## PROBLEM: You have a rare STI and so do your colleagues

 You have just had your annual medical exam. The doctor informs you that you have a rare STI. There are others who have contracted it – all your colleagues of the opposite sex in the company. The doctor will quickly deduct who is to blame for this pandemic.

## SOLUTION: The man who could not speak

1. Relax; the doctor is bound by doctor-patient confidentiality.
2. Take advantage of it and confide in him. Give him all the details of how you have bonked so-and-so. It will do you good to share.
3. Tell him, for example: "I've bonked my assistant in the boss's office at least five times, and I don't answer her e-mails any more."
4. Tell him also that you exhausted the intern so much that she had to take unpaid leave.
5. Don't forget to ask for the pills to treat your STI.

## Expert Opinion

"By the way, if the doctor starts the physical by asking how you feel in the company, answer: 'Great, I bonk every three days!' He will tick 'In great shape' in your medical file."

## Testimonial

"I panicked and said that I had a virus on my computer and that it must be linked. The doctor just sighed..." Judy, Interpreter, Inverness

## PROBLEM: The colleague you bonked writes about it on your Facebook wall

You bonked a colleague at work. The next day you open Facebook to find out that the idiot wrote on your wall: "Thank you for the wonderful bonk last night in the meeting room!" The information has already made three rounds of the company.

## SOLUTION: Surprise!

1. Don't delete the message from your wall. It's too late; everyone has seen it. The only solution that works in such situations is to reveal something even worse, which will completely overshadow the fact that you bonked in the meeting room.
2. Respond to the message on the wall with the following: "You're welcome, but you hadn't told me that you had three nipples!" or "I would have never pegged you as someone who has a tattoo of their boss's face on the small of your back..."
3. The information about the bonk will be drowned under a flurry of comments from the idiot's friends and colleagues.
4. Take said idiot off your friend list.

## Expert Opinion

"Create a Facebook group 'I love to bonk at work'. This is an excellent way to meet new partners.'

## Testimonial

"When a colleague saw I had bonked the hot assistant, he created the "I bonked Miss X" group. 15 colleagues have already joined." Pietro, File Clerk, Milan

## PROBLEM: You are caught *in flagrante* and risk being fired

 You bonked at work and were caught in the act. You have to face a disciplinary panel consisting of very conservative members from management. You risk losing your job.

## SOLUTION: A proven method

1. Go to the hearing dressed elegantly, sit down and look solemn.
2. Look into the eyes of the commission members one by one and say: "I want to say one thing to the people of this company, and I want you to listen to me."
3. Raise your index finger and say: "I DID NOT. HAVE. SEXUAL. RELATIONS WITH THAT WOMAN. MISS LEWINSKY."
   Note: Instead of "Miss Lewinsky" use the name of the colleague you bonked.
4. Add: "These allegations are false."
5. Finish by saying: "And I need to go back to work for the people of this company. Thank you."
6. Leave during the panel's rapturous applause.

## Expert Opinion

"Don't bring your mother to make the commission cry; you are not in the classroom and you are not eight years old."

## Testimonial

"I didn't evaluate the situation well. As there were four of us in the room, I suggested a group bonk. I was fired." Iain, Court Reporter, Blackpool

**Fig 1. Work Diagram**

SALARY

PROMOTION

WORKING HARD

**Fig 2. Bonk Diagram**

SALARY

POWER

CAREER

PROMOTION

**BONKING HARD**

RELAXATION

SEDUCTION

EFFICIENCY

MONEY

## Expert Opinion

"You can get what you want at work in two ways: you can work hard or you can bonk hard. Different methods, but the results are very similar. Choose yours according to your own vision of how you want to spend your days at work."

# PART 6: HOW TO IMPROVE YOUR WORK LIFE BY BONKING AT WORK

What does it take for you to finally come to work happy and eager?

How to get everything you ever wanted in your company.
How to create your dream team.

Find out in the next pages that working until 10 pm every day, including Sundays, is not necessarily the best way to get promoted in your career.

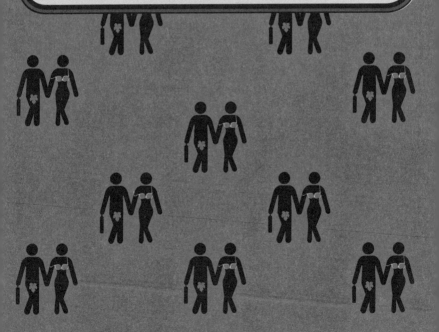

# THE BASICS

## Maslow pyramid

**SELF ACTUALIZATION**
You have
bonked all
of your colleagues.

**ESTEEM**
You can get a 50% or more
success rate when you simply
ask a colleague: "Shall we bonk?"

**BELONGING**
You have the opportunity to pick-up colleagues in the firm
during lunch time, in the open-space or in the tea room.

**SAFETY**
You have a job with enough
hidden bonk spots.

**PHYSIOLOGICAL**
You know where the canteen and the tea room are
and where you can rest at work.

## Test your work bonking skills

Bonking at work can improve your work life if you do it right. It is time to find out if you understood the philosophy and the power of the tips we gave you in this book.

## I WANT...
## a longer lunch break

A) I ask my boss for a longer lunch break.
B) I always eat with my boss who eats out and takes a longer lunch break than the common employees.
C) I go and eat out with my boss and I bonk him/her at the restaurant. He/she will not be mad at me if I come back from my lunch break late.

## I WANT...
## to eliminate a colleague who is my competition for the same post / for a promotion?

A) I ask my boss to limit the number of applicants for the post to just one: me.
B) I break my colleague's computer with a chair the minute he/she finishes an important project.
C) I start a rumour that he/she drunk-bonked the ugliest person in accounts on the office photocopier.

## I WANT...
### to be sure to get my own office

A) I ask my boss if I could please have my own office.
B) I fashion my own cubicle out of cardboard.
C) I bonk shamelessly all over the building until management suggests I get an office.

## I DON'T WANT...
### to be bored during
### after-work drinks

A) I talk to my boss the whole time.
B) I put a plastic cup on my nose and imitate a pig to amuse my colleagues.
C) I take advantage of my colleagues when they are drunk and bonk them back at the office.

## I WANT...
### to supplement my income

A) I ask my boss for a raise.
B) I sell my office furniture on eBay.
C) I take a second job as a sex hotline operator during office hours.

## I WANT...
### more time off

A) I ask my boss for some time off.
B) I come back from holiday two weeks late, explaining that my watch stopped working.
C) I bonk the person in HR in charge of allocating vacation days.

## I WANT...
### to have a work accident and be paid huge compensation

A) I don't waste anyone's time and ask for the compensation directly.
B) I throw myself from the top of a tall cupboard onto my PC monitor.
C) I intentionally hurt myself with the zip of my trousers and accuse my boss of having bit me.

## I WANT...
### to make my colleague do my work

A) I ask my boss if my colleague could do my work.
B) I ask my colleague loudly and decisively to kindly do my work.
C) I make him/her my sex slave and make him/her do my work.

## I AM...
## a man and want my female boss's job

A) I ask my boss for her job.
B) I bring studies to work which prove that women are less competent.
C) I bonk her, make her pregnant, and while she's away on her maternity leave I take her place and show everyone that I do a better job.

## I WANT...
## new male colleagues

A) I ask my boss to hire new male colleagues.
B) I invent new posts and publish ads for them on the internet; ads mention that there is free beer and football during lunch breaks.
C) I start a rumour that my company is creating a porn production dept.

## I WANT...
## to get rid of the colleagues I don't like

A) I ask my boss if these people could be fired.
B) I print and send letters of dismissal to the colleagues that I don't like.
C) I organise a group bonk with these persons and invite the management to witness it.

## I AM...
## a woman and want my male boss's job

A) I ask my boss for his job.
B) I bring studies to work which prove that women really are more competent.
C) I send an invitation for a group bonk from his computer to all the female employees in his department, copying the HR department.

## I WANT...
## new female colleagues

A) I ask my boss to hire new female colleagues.
B) I invent new posts and publish ads for them on the internet; the ads mention that there are designer freebies given out every lunch break.
C) I impregnate all the girls on the team.

## I WANT...
## to get rid of an annoying auditor

A) I ask my boss to make the mean auditor leave.
B) I repeat everything like a parrot.
C) I buy my peace by giving him a database consisting of all the names and characteristics of the most bonkalicious employees in the company.

## I WANT...
### to know if my boss is into S&M

A) I simply ask my boss if he likes S&M.
B) I check my boss's Intranet profile to see if he has marked S&M under Hobbies.
C) I discreetly whip him with a mouse cable during a meeting and observe his reaction.

## I WANT...
### to improve my relationship with the boss's PA

A) I ask my boss to let me attend a social relations course.
B) I give him/her chocolate.
C) I bonk him/her regularly.

## I WANT...
### a company mobile phone

A) I ask my boss for a mobile phone.
B) I give my phone bill and my family's phone bill to accounts and demand that it be paid forthwith.
C) I bonk the person who allocates company mobile phones.

## I DON'T WANT...
### to be bored at work

A) I ask my boss to give me more to do.
B) I buy a yo-yo.
C) I invite my lover to work and tell everyone he/she is an important client of the company.

## I WANT...
### to relax before an important, stressful meeting

A) I ask my boss for tips on how to relax.
B) I sleep on my keyboard for 30 minutes before the meeting.
C) I discreetly masturbate prior to the meeting to release endorphins.

## I WANT...
### to leave work earlier every day

A) I ask my boss if I can leave earlier.
B) I say I have taken up evening courses of playing the trumpet on a pony.
C) I organize a daily bonk for my boss towards the end of the day so that I can leave as soon as he gets busy in his office.

## I WANT..
## to work from home
## (so that I can work less)

A) I ask my boss if he would mind if I work from home, so that I could work less.
B) I don't wash for a month.
C) I promise my boss I will use the time at home to make innovative hand-made sex toys and send them to him discreetly.

## I DON'T WANT...
## to be bored any more
## in meetings

A) I talk to my boss.
B) I organize a race around the table on chairs on wheels.
C) I propose a group bonk among all team members in the name of team-building.

## I WANT...
## a better computer

A) I ask my boss for a better computer.
B) I take someone else's computer that I like.
C) I give an 800Gb disk of porn to the head of IT.

## I WANT...
## to finally find something interesting
## on the Intranet

A) I ask my boss to let me take a course on how to use the Intranet.
B) I suggest that the Intranet be transformed into the Internet because it would make it more interesting.
C) I ask the IT person to show me how to do sexy webcam video chats with colleagues via the Intranet.

## I WANT...
## a company car

A) I ask my boss for a car.
B) I steal the keys of one of the company cars.
C) I bonk the person who allocates company cars.

|   | 6 | 7 | 8 | 9 | 10 | SUB TOTAL |
|---|---|---|---|---|---|---|
| A |   |   |   |   |   |   |
| B |   |   |   |   |   |   |
| C |   |   |   |   |   |   |

|   | 6 | 7 | 8 | 9 | 10 | SUB TOTAL |
|---|---|---|---|---|---|---|
| A |   |   |   |   |   |   |
| B |   |   |   |   |   |   |
| C |   |   |   |   |   |   |

|   | 6 | 7 | 8 | 9 | 10 | SUB TOTAL |
|---|---|---|---|---|---|---|
| A |   |   |   |   |   |   |
| B |   |   |   |   |   |   |
| C |   |   |   |   |   |   |

|   | 6 | 7 | 8 | 9 | 10 | SUB TOTAL |
|---|---|---|---|---|---|---|
| A |   |   |   |   |   |   |
| B |   |   |   |   |   |   |
| C |   |   |   |   |   |   |

|   | 6 | 7 | 8 | 9 | 10 | SUB TOTAL |
|---|---|---|---|---|---|---|
| A |   |   |   |   |   |   |
| B |   |   |   |   |   |   |
| C |   |   |   |   |   |   |

**GRAND TOTAL**

As _____    Bs _____    Cs _____

## You mostly answered A

We bet that you asked your boss permission to read this book. You have a highly developed sense of hierarchy, but you are focusing too much on your boss and will never achieve much. Try to put into practice the few pages in this book that you do understand.

## You answered mostly B

You have some imagination and can think outside the box. This is very good, but unfortunately you have not yet understood the potential of workplace bonking. This book will help you, but only if you trust us completely and make an effort to follow our advice.

## You answered mostly C

Bravo, you are a good student of *How to Bonk at Work*. Your open spirit and capacity to follow advice from this book will take you far in your career! You can contact us to participate in the creation of the sequel to this book.

# PART 7: HOW TO MAKE SEX TOYS OUT OF OFFICE SUPPLIES

Want to spice up your bonking at the company's expense?
Want to make the latest sex toys yourself?
Want to relax with some manual activities during office hours?

Find out in the following pages how a roll of tape and two paper clips can inject sensuality into your office hours.

# THE BASICS

## The Laptop Law

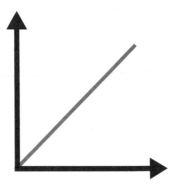

% of company laptops equipped with a webcam

Number of amateur office porn films available on the internet

Manufacturers of office supplies have found that 12% of their products are used to make sex toys. This figure is rapidly increasing now that sex toys have become far more commonplace.

## Office Supplies

 For sex toys     For work

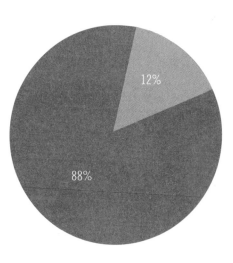

# How to make a 'Bad Boy/Bad Girl' tool kit

## You Will Need:

Several rubber stamps
1 to 3 paper clips

## Duration:

10 minutes

**Step 1**
Get several rubber stamps from the office supply room.

**Step 2**
Undress.

**Step 3**
Stamp yourself in bad boy
places (biceps, shoulder,
neck...).

**Step 4**
Stamp other areas too, but don't
forget to do it upside down so
people can't read "Approved",
"Received", "Accounts" or other
turn-offs.

**Step 5**
Clip a paperclip to your genitals
to make it look like you have a
piercing.

# How to make a nice panther mask

## You Will Need:

1 sheet of paper
50 cm (20 in) of string
1 pair of scissors
1 marking pen

## Duration:

7 minutes

**Step 1**
Print a panther motif on an
A4 sheet of paper.

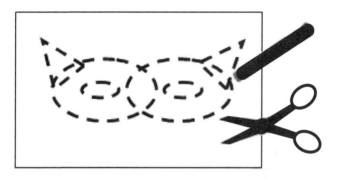

**Step 2**
Draw panther eyes and cut them out.

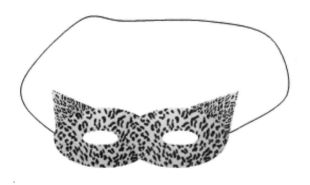

**Step 3**
Attach the string and place the mask on your head.

# How to make a vibrating ring with a roll of tape

## You Will Need:

1 roll of tape
1 mobile phone
1 regular phone

## Duration:

4 minutes

**Step 1**
Take the tape.

**Step 2**
Take your mobile phone and set it on vibrating mode.

**Step 3**
Tape the phone to the roll
of tape.

**Step 4**
Slip on the roll, return to
your desk and call yourself.

## How to fashion sex handcuffs from material in your office

### You Will Need:

2 large rolls of tape
1 mouse (with wire)
1 pair of scissors

### Duration:

3 minutes

**x2**

**Step 1**
Get the two rolls ready.

**Step 2**
Cut off the wire from
the mouse.

**Step 3**
Link the two rolls
with the wire.

# How to make a spanking paddle with your keyboard

## You Will Need:

1 regular phone
1 keyboard
1 roll of scotch tape

## Duration:

5 minutes

**Step 1**
Take the keyboard.

**Step 2**
Unplug the handset
from the phone.

**Step 3**
Tape the two together,
as shown.

## How to make a whip

### You Will Need:

1 pencil
1 pair of scissors
5 thumbtacks
1 piece of fabric (curtains, shirt…)
Some tape

### Duration:

5 minutes

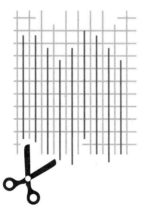

**Step 1**
Cut the fabric into
five strips.

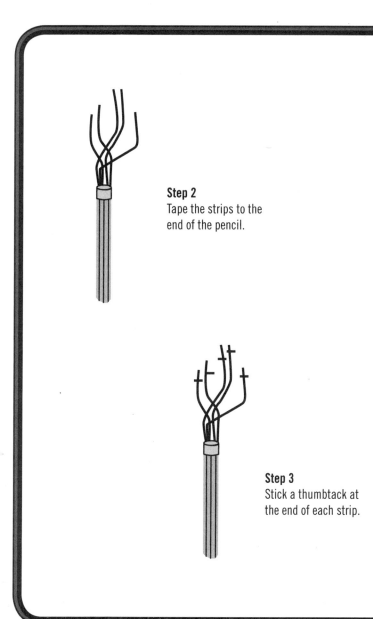

**Step 2**
Tape the strips to the
end of the pencil.

**Step 3**
Stick a thumbtack at
the end of each strip.

# How to make a pair of nipple clamps

## You Will Need:

2 paper clamps
60 cm (2 ft) of packing string

## Duration:

2 minutes

**Step 1**
Cut the string into two
pieces, 30 cm (1 ft) long.

**Step 2**
Tie the two clamps together with a piece of string.

**Step 3**
Tie the two pieces of string toegther,
as indicated.

**Step 4**
Place each clamp on a nipple and the remaining
string in your mouth.

# Bonk Bonus

## Annual bonk planner

For each week, put the name of the colleague(s) you plan to bonk.

| week 1 | week 2 | week 3 | week 4 |
|---|---|---|---|
| M | M | M | M |
| T | T | T | T |
| W | W | W | W |
| T | T | T | T |
| F | F | F | F |

| week 5 | week 6 | week 7 | week 8 |
|---|---|---|---|
| M | M | M | M |
| T | T | T | T |
| W | W | W | W |
| T | T | T | T |
| F | F | F | F |

| week 9 | week 10 | week 11 | week 12 |
|---|---|---|---|
| M | M | M | M |
| T | T | T | T |
| W | W | W | W |
| T | T | T | T |
| F | F | F | F |

| week 13 | week 14 | week 15 | week 16 |
|---|---|---|---|
| M | M | M | M |
| T | T | T | T |
| W | W | W | W |
| T | T | T | T |
| F | F | F | F |

| week 17 | week 18 | week 19 | week 20 |
|---|---|---|---|
| M | M | M | M |
| T | T | T | T |
| W | W | W | W |
| T | T | T | T |
| F | F | F | F |

| week 21 | week 22 | week 23 | week 24 |
|---|---|---|---|
| M | M | M | M |
| T | T | T | T |
| W | W | W | W |
| T | T | T | T |
| F | F | F | F |

| week 25 | week 26 | week 27 | week 28 |
|---|---|---|---|
| M | M | M | M |
| T | T | T | T |
| W | W | W | W |
| T | T | T | T |
| F | F | F | F |

| week 29 | week 30 | week 31 | week 32 |
|---|---|---|---|
| M | M | M | M |
| T | T | T | T |
| W | W | W | W |
| T | T | T | T |
| F | F | F | F |

| week 33 | week 34 | week 35 | week 36 |
|---|---|---|---|
| M | M | M | M |
| I | T | T | T |
| W | W | W | W |
| T | T | T | T |
| F | F | F | F |

| week 37 | week 38 | week 39 | week 40 |
|---|---|---|---|
| M | M | M | M |
| T | T | T | T |
| W | W | W | W |
| T | T | T | T |
| F | F | F | F |

| week 41 | week 42 | week 43 | week 44 |
|---|---|---|---|
| M | M | M | M |
| T | T | T | T |
| W | W | W | W |
| T | T | T | T |
| F | F | F | F |

| week 45 | week 46 | week 47 | week 48 |
|---|---|---|---|
| M | M | M | M |
| T | T | T | T |
| W | W | W | W |
| T | T | T | T |
| F | F | F | F |

| week 49 | week 50 | week 51 | week 52 |
|---|---|---|---|
| M | M | M | M |
| T | T | T | T |
| W | W | W | W |
| T | T | T | T |
| F | F | F | F |

## Bonk Bonus

### Bonk at Work notes